MORE BRIGHT SPARKS

© ALISTAIR SMITH
ISBN 1-85539-148-1

Production by AL!TE
45 Wycombe End, Beaconsfield, Bucks HP9 1LZ

Design & Layout: Neil Hawkins, NEP
Published by: Network Educational Press Ltd
Illustrations: Oliver Caviglioli
Printed in Great Britain by MPG Books Ltd

MORE BRIGHT SPARKS

contents

MORE BRIGHT SPARKS

an introduction

The posters in this book are designed for use with young learners. You may choose to use them in a school classroom or corridor, in the reception area or in your own home. The posters are carefully chosen and organized to convey different sorts of learning messages. There are messages about positive attitude, guidance from role models, provocative questions about thinking and creativity and simple instructions on becoming a good learner.

Can you teach creativity? If so, what would creativity lessons look like? As soon as one puts the words 'teach', 'creativity' and 'lessons' together in the same sentence something begins to feel wrong. Creativity involves breaking patterns of thought, expectation or behaviour. Creativity involves the generation of the new. In order to break patterns one must first of all understand the patterns. Surely, then, we need to lay down some rules and some understanding before we disrupt the creative process.

I suppose I could teach disruption. I've certainly presided over upheaval in my past as a classroom teacher, but none of it was planned and very little creativity was developed as a consequence. Intelligent behaviour involves the early recognition of patterns, the seeking and securing of connections, some of which are near and some of which are far, and it also involves identifying categories.

For young learners, encouraging and nurturing their creativity is more difficult than it sounds. At face value it would appear that imitation, mimicry and play – natural dispositions in the naïve learner and framed by millions of years of evolutionary development – are the very core of learning and of creativity. All we therefore need to do is structure more of it and make it less life threatening. In the natural world the classroom is a dangerous environment: a very high percentage of seal pup deaths occur in play. Provided we take care to make play safe for young learners, then we might expect creativity to be developed as a consequence. This feral approach will disappoint. To push a boundary one must have an understanding of the boundary. It needn't be a shared understanding or the commonly accepted understanding, but it must have a recognized starting point.

Creativity cannot be developed in a vacuum. It is argued that if it can be taught, then it can only be taught within a context. Creativity cannot usefully be timetabled for Thursday afternoon. The challenge is to saturate everyday learning experiences with creative opportunities. To do so in a generic way is hopelessly idealistic. Some children journey in tiny and predictable footsteps while others leap with random energy. Good learning, like good creativity, occurs with a high level of personal responsibility, opportunities to reflect, to make new meanings and to redirect oneself and one's thinking as a consequence. Young learners need assistance in doing this. In the natural world this assistance is known as a parent. In the world of formal learning we call it a teacher.

The teacher nurtures creativity and independence of learning by making it safe to take risks and by creating the best conditions for experimentation. Not easy with 32 six year olds. Active independence – 32 six year olds doing their own thing as and how they please – is fools' gold, but independence of thought, creative and imaginative thinking, is not. The posters in this book are carefully chosen to encourage individual children to recognize that a set of attributes needs to be developed to become a good learner. We call them the 5 Rs.

The first of the 5 Rs is Resilience. Resilience involves persisting in the face of difficulty and being disposed to do so rather than give up. Learners who are resilient focus on performance rather than outcome. They say things like, 'How do I get better?' and are less likely to make comparisons with other, better, performers. Teachers do a lot to develop resilience by encouraging performance improvement strategies rather than a focus on raw scores. Our Resilience posters are drawn largely from role models who have shown the value of persistence and 'stickability' in their lives. Teacher feedback that praises for specific performance improvements, including marking which gives bullet points for improvement, demonstrates the power of little by little improvements.

The second of the 5 Rs is Responsibility. Formal learning occurs alongside others and the young learner needs to show consideration for the learning needs of others. In some instances this may mean familiarity with some ground rules for learning such as asking good questions, exhibiting good listening, and showing tolerance and consideration. Responsible learners understand that their needs operate within the needs of a larger group which is called 'our class'.

To be resolute and responsible is not enough if you are, at the same time, inflexible. Our next of the 5 Rs is Resourcefulness. To be resourceful is to know, or have an instinct for knowing, what to do next. This may mean knowing what to do when you get stuck. It may mean knowing how to think when you reach a dead end. It may mean knowing the best questions to ask and how to ask them. Resourceful learners are those who have been inspired by your model to be confident in their creative and problem-solving approaches and they are prepared to take risks in their own learning.

To be able to reason means that you will eventually appreciate the complexity of learning and understand that not all questions have answers. Our fourth of the 5 Rs is Reasoning. We encourage this by posing problems and by encouraging different categories of thinking. To be able to reason requires learners to gather evidence, to break down problems, to weigh evidence, to assemble pros and cons, to speculate and hypothesize, and to shift their thinking across different modes. Our posters encourage this by moving from the abstract to the concrete and from the imaginary to the real.

The best learners reflect. It is through reflection that habits are changed. Our fifth of the 5 Rs is Reflection. You will find posters that are less direct, more philosophical, more likely to challenge patterns of thought and test values. Learning occurs when thinking time has been structured in such a way to allow reflection on past behaviours and connect them to a possible new set of behaviours. Good teachers facilitate this; many of our posters will help in this process.

The 5 Rs are described in *The ALPS Approach Resource Book* and owe their origin to work done by Guy Claxton and described in his book *Wise Up*.

What other uses can be found for these posters? Our 5 Rs are like a well rehearsed boy (or girl) band. Each offers a different set of attributes; each could have their own promising career but they work better singing together and in harmony. At a practical level you can dip into them and choose a theme for the week, exhibit the theme in the school parent newsletter, talk it up in assembly time, post it around the school. Use designated spaces on classroom walls for the theme or thought or question of the week. Encourage learners to put responses and thoughts on sticky notes in that same space. Do something similar in corridors. Use the posters as raw material for screen saver messages on computers. Place them as scrolling quotes on your website. Hang them suspended as mobiles above your desk. Encourage children to provide their own, to copy them and place them on the fridge at home, to say why they like them and why they are important. Use the posters as prompts for circle time discussion. Share your own favourites with your class

I hope you find these posters challenging, intriguing and useful, and that you find creative ways of using them. Remember learning is more fun than fun...

Alistair Smith, February 2003

MORE BRIGHT SPARKS

RESILIENCE

'If you think you won't do well – why not surprise yourself?'

MORE BR!GHT SPARKS

'Change your bad habits before your bad habits change you.'

MORE BRIGHT SPARKS

'No one can make you feel bad about yourself unless you let them...'

MORE BR!GHT SPARKS

'If you are not big enough to lose, then you are not big enough to win.'

MORE BR!GHT SPARKS

'To be
the best –
self-test!'

MORE BRIGHT SPARKS

'Your focus is your reality.'

Star Wars 1 – The Phantom Menace

MORE BR!GHT SPARKS

'Unless you stand for something, you will fall for anything.'

MORE BRIGHT SPARKS

'Doing what's right isn't always easy, but it's always right.'

MORE BRIGHT SPARKS

'The spirited horse, which will try to win the race of its own accord, will run even faster if encouraged.'

Ovid, c AD9

MORE BRIGHT SPARKS

'To be number one you have to train like you are number two.'

Maurice Green, US sprinter

'Nothing is impossible.'

Christopher Reeve, actor, best known as Superman,
paralysed by an accident in 1995

'Preparation prevents poor performance.'

MORE BR!GHT SPARKS

'Whatever
you do,
don't do it
halfway.'

Bob Beamon, former Olympic athlete and world
record holder for the long jump

MORE BRIGHT SPARKS

'Good enough rarely is.'

'Champions aren't made in gyms. Champions are made from something they have deep inside them – a desire, a dream, a vision. They have to have the skill, and the will. But the will must be stronger than the skill.'

Muhammad Ali

'Love what's lovable and hate what's hateable – it takes brains to see the difference.'

Robert Frost, poet

'Can you
step into the
same river
twice?'

MORE BRIGHT SPARKS

'Is there a use for used confetti?'

MORE BRIGHT SPARKS

'Prefix has no suffix.

But suffix has a prefix.'

'If sign makers go on strike – who writes their signs?'

MORE BRIGHT SPARKS

'Hold a shoe to your ear – can you hear the footsteps?'

MORE BR!GHT SPARKS

‘Why don't sheep shrink when it rains?’

'Would lightning be faster if it didn't zigzag?'

MORE BRIGHT SPARKS

'Learning is more fun than fun.'

Noel Coward

MORE BRIGHT SPARKS

'Wake up like you've never woken up before!'

'Believe in miracles but don't depend on them.'

MORE BR!GHT SPARKS

'Be a super human.'

MORE BRIGHT SPARKS

'Don't just be honest, be honest and be just.'

MORE BRIGHT SPARKS

RESPONSIBILITY

MORE
BR!GHT
SPARKS

'Success is all a matter of luck – ask any failure.'

MORE BRIGHT SPARKS

'Success comes before work only in the dictionary.'

Anonymous

MORE BRIGHT SPARKS

'You cannot shake hands with a clenched fist.'

Indira Gandhi

MORE BRIGHT SPARKS

Three rules for making and keeping friends:

- see the best in them
- be your best for them
- share your best with them

MORE BRIGHT SPARKS

Five things to do before asking the teacher for a spelling:

1. Use the table dictionary.
2. Use the class dictionary.
3. Use a spelling log.
4. Use your 'have a go' book.
5. Ask a friend or another adult.

MORE BRIGHT SPARKS

Five things to do before asking the teacher to read a word:

1. Look at the pictures.
2. Read the rest of the sentence.
3. Look at the letters and blend the sounds.
4. Is it like any other word you know?
5. Ask a friend.

MORE BRIGHT SPARKS

To do good 'lining up' you must:

- Face the front.

- Put your arms by your sides.

- Keep your feet still.

- Be quiet and be ready to listen.

A good listener:

- Looks at the person who is talking.

- Thinks carefully about what is being said.

- Asks a question if they don't understand.

MORE BRIGHT SPARKS

Good questions:

- help you understand

- help you get better

- help you become a good thinker

MORE BRIGHT SPARKS

It's your temper! Please keep it.

MORE BRIGHT SPARKS

'Are you a bully?

Or a buddy?'

MORE BRIGHT SPARKS

'Notice what distracts you and plan to avoid it.'

'Just because you disagree with someone doesn't mean you have to be disagreeable.'

MORE BRIGHT SPARKS

'With a minute of anger you lose sixty seconds of happiness.'

MORE BR!GHT SPARKS

'Your
future
begins
today.'

MORE BRIGHT SPARKS

'Who you are begins with how you are.'

MORE BRIGHT SPARKS

'Never put a drink on a book.'

MORE BR!GHT SPARKS

'Never sharpen a boomerang.'

MORE BRIGHT SPARKS

'Your conscience is your little voice that wonders, "is somebody looking?"'

MORE BR!GHT SPARKS

'Don't trample on too many toes –

you may want to kiss them tomorrow!'

MORE BR!GHT SPARKS

'Doing the
thing right –
is doing the
right thing.'

MORE BR!GHT SPARKS

'A little virtue won't hurt you.'

MORE
BRIGHT
SPARKS

'You can fail many times, but you don't become a failure until you blame somebody else.'

MORE
BR!GHT
SPARKS

RESOURCEFULNESS

MORE BRIGHT SPARKS

'The best learners ask the best questions: how good are yours?'

MORE BRIGHT SPARKS

'Together Everyone Achieves More.'

MORE BRIGHT SPARKS

'Creativity is when you make a connection no one has thought of before.'

'In the end you get more from what you give than what you get.'

MORE BRIGHT SPARKS

'As soon as you get up in the morning remind yourself how good you are.'

MORE BR!GHT SPARKS

'Creativity is doing things differently –
or doing the same things but in a different way.'

'Use all the brains you have and all you can borrow.'

MORE BR!GHT SPARKS

‘You don’t take medicine in the dark.’

MORE
BR!GHT
SPARKS

'I dream for a living.'

Steven Spielberg, film director and producer

MORE BRIGHT SPARKS

'Discovery consists in seeing what everyone else has seen and thinking what no one else has thought.'

Albert Szent-Gyorgyi,
Nobel Prize winning biochemist

Good genius questions:

What?
Where?
Who?
When?
Why?

Four steps to being creative:

1. collect lots of ideas
2. use these ideas in your head
3. select the most exciting
4. bring it to life

MORE BRIGHT SPARKS

'Creativity involves breaking out of established patterns in order to look at things in a different way.'

Edward De Bono

MORE BR!GHT SPARKS

'A mistake is simply another way of doing things.'

MORE BR!GHT SPARKS

'Anyone can make a mistake. A fool insists on repeating it.'

MORE BRIGHT SPARKS

'There are two kinds of people in the world – bath people and shower people.'

Yoko Ono

MORE BRIGHT SPARKS

'It's better to do only one good thing in life than 18 average ones.'

Ricky Gervais, comedian and star of hit television show *The Office*

MORE BRIGHT SPARKS

'If a man is called to be a street-sweeper, he should sweep streets even as Michelangelo painted, or Beethoven composed music, or Shakespeare wrote poetry. He should sweep streets so well that all the hosts of heaven and earth will pause to say, "Here lived a great street-sweeper who did his job well".'

Martin Luther King Jr.

MORE BRIGHT SPARKS

'To do the right thing, at the right time, in the right way; to do some things better than they were ever done before; to eliminate errors; to know both sides of the question; to be courteous; to be an example; to love our work; to anticipate requirements; to develop resources; to recognize no impediments; to master circumstances; to act from reason rather than rule; to be satisfied with nothing short of perfection.'

Marshall Field & Company, US retail store

'People forget how fast you did a job, but they remember how well you did it.'

Howard W. Newton, US writer

'If you do things well, do them better. Be daring, be first, be different, be just.'

Anita Roddick OBE, founder of The Body Shop

MORE BR!GHT SPARKS

'Think
Believe
Dream
Dare.'

MORE
BRIGHT
SPARKS

'Making the simple complicated is commonplace; making the complicated simple, awesomely simple, that's creativity.'

Charlie Mingus, jazz musician

MORE BRIGHT SPARKS

'Flaming enthusiasm, backed by common sense and persistence, is the quality that most frequently makes for success.'

Dale Carnegie

MORE BRIGHT SPARKS

'I don't know the key to success, but the key to failure is trying to please everybody.'

Bill Cosby

MORE BR!GHT SPARKS

'Eighty
per cent of
success is
showing up.'

Woody Allen

REASONING

'Whenever two people meet there are really six people present: each man as he sees himself, as the other person sees him, and as he really is.'

William James, US philospher

MORE BRIGHT SPARKS

'He who knows all the answers has not yet been asked all the questions.'

Unknown

'A horse is outside a saloon bar, tied to a piece of rope five metres long. There is a bale of hay six metres away from the horse. If the horse is tied to a piece of rope that is only five metres long, how come the horse can eat the hay whenever it wants?'

MORE BRIGHT SPARKS

'A man fell out of an aeroplane. He didn't land in water, a tree, a haystack or on a mattress. In fact, he landed on the ground and nothing cushioned his fall. Apart from a sprained ankle, he survived. How come?'

'If it takes three minutes to boil one egg, how long will it take to boil six eggs?'

MORE BRIGHT SPARKS

'What is it that occurs four times in every week, twice in every month and only once in a year?'

'You have two coins that add up to 55p. One of them can't be a 5p piece. What are the two coins?'

'I arrive home just as I hear the clock striking one. Half an hour later the clock strikes one again. Half an hour later the clock strikes one again. Half an hour later the clock strikes one again. What time was it when I came home?'

'A cowboy rode into a western town on Friday, stayed for three days and two nights, without ever leaving the town, and rode out again on Friday. How come?'

'Before Mount Everest was discovered which was the highest mountain in the world?'

REFLECTION

MORE
BR!GHT
SPARKS

'You don't have to be a cow to know what milk is – make sure you can use your imagination!'

'He who learns, and makes no use of his learning, is a beast of burden with a load of books. Does the ass comprehend whether he carries on his back a library or a bundle of wood?'

Moslih Eddin Saadi (1184–1291), Persian poet

MORE BRIGHT SPARKS

'Between the optimist and the pessimist The difference is droll: The optimist sees the doughnut But the pessimist sees the hole.'

McLandburgh Wilson, US writer

MORE BR!GHT SPARKS

'Television is an electrical device which, when turned off, stimulates conversation.'

MORE BRIGHT SPARKS

'56 per cent of statistics are made up on the spot.'

MORE BR!GHT SPARKS

'Mistakes are like scraps of fertilizer scattered through our lives. They encourage us to grow and sprout new leaves.'

Mariella Frostrup, television presenter and actress

'There are two mistakes one can make along the road to truth – not going all the way, and not starting.'

Buddha

'Exams are very similar to football – three rules: preparation, preparation, preparation.'

Jamie Theakston, television presenter

MORE BRIGHT SPARKS

'Someone once said to me, "First identify your obsession, then make it your profession and you will never do another day's work".'

Rolf Harris, television personality

MORE BR!GHT SPARKS

'If you have a dream you can make it happen.'

Ellen MacArthur, round the world yachtswoman

'A man in this world without learning is as a beast of the field.'

Hindu proverb

MORE BRIGHT SPARKS

'The bully says,
"Go!"
the friend
says,
"Let's go!"'

MORE BRIGHT SPARKS

'He who is afraid to ask is ashamed of learning.'

Danish proverb

MORE BRIGHT SPARKS

'The mind is like a muscle – it has to be trained.'

Sven Goran-Ericksson, football manager

MORE BRIGHT SPARKS

'My father told me to learn the piano and that way I'd always get invited to parties.'

Sir Paul McCartney

'I try to do the right
thing at the right time.
They may just be little
things, but usually
they make the
difference between
winning and losing.'

Kareem Abdul-Jabar, US basketball player

'Two roads diverged
in a wood, and I
took the one less
travelled by.
And that has made
all the difference.'

Robert Frost, poet

'I'd like to be a bigger and more knowledgeable person ten years from now than I am today. I think, as we grow older, we must discipline ourselves to continue expanding, broadening, learning, keeping our minds active and open.'

Clint Eastwood, US actor and director

MORE BRIGHT SPARKS

Practise exam technique in your head – imagine you...

1. sit down, make yourself comfortable and look around...

2. breathe deeply and relax...

3. open the exam paper and flick through, a page at a time, to the end, then breathe deeply...

4. read the questions and look at the marks for each...

5. write down the time to spend on each question alongside...

6. map a quick answer with keywords for each question and...

7. successfully answer all the questions – and pass the exam!

10 suggestions for schools using these posters

1. Display above eye level in classrooms and around the school.
2. Display in classrooms, in a designated space, as a theme for the week.
3. Use as a teaching tool for discussion, for example asking children to choose their favourite saying and explaining why it is important to them.
4. Encourage children to copy the posters and stick them up at home.
5. Use as screen savers on the school computer network.
6. Put into pupil planners and homework diaries.
7. Use as a theme for an assembly or for a series of 'learning to learn' assemblies.
8. Put onto the school website.
9. Put into the parent newsletter and explain how they can be used at home.
10. Use as a staff development tool. Include posters in staffrooms and encourage staff to explore ways of using the posters with pupils and developing the theme throughout their teaching.

MORE BRIGHT SPARKS

Acknowledgements

Quote by Christopher Reeve. *Nothing is Impossible* by Christopher Reeve published by Century. Used by permission of The Random House Group Limited.

Quote from Noel Coward. Reproduced by permission of Ali Howarth on behalf of Alan Brodie Representation, authorized representatives of the Estate of Noel Coward.

Quote by Steven Spielberg. Reproduced by permission of Gerry Lewis on behalf of Steven Spielberg.

Quote by Edward De Bono. Reproduced by permission of Diana McQuaig on behalf of The McQuaig Group Inc.

Quote by Yoko Ono. Reproduced by permission of Jonas Herbsman on behalf of Yoko Ono.

Quote by Ricky Gervais. Reproduced by permission of Duncan Hayes on behalf of Ricky Gervais.

Quote from Marshall Field & Company. Courtesy of Marshall Field's.

Quote by Anita Roddick. Reproduced by permission of Karen Bishop on behalf of Anita Roddick Publications Ltd.

Quote from Dale Carnegie. Reproduced by permission of Arnold Jay Gitomer, attorney-at-law for Donna Dale Carnegie.

Quote by Mariella Frostrup. Reproduced by permission of Debbie Catchpole at John Noel Management on behalf of Mariella Frostrup.

Quote by Jamie Theakston. Reproduced by permission of Michael Foster at Artists' Rights Group Ltd on behalf of Jamie Theakston.

Acknowledgements

Quote by Rolf Harris. Reproduced by permission of Tony Peake on behalf of Rolf Harris.

Quote by Ellen MacArthur. Taken from Ellen MacArthur's autobiography *Taking on the World* available at www.ellenmacarthur.com; reproduced by permission of A.P. Watt Ltd on behalf of Offshore Challenges Ltd.

Quote by Sven Goran-Ericksson. Reproduced by permission of Clive Richards on behalf of Sven Goran-Ericksson.

Quote by Sir Paul McCartney. Reproduced by permission of Lilian Marshall at MPL Communications Inc. on behalf of Sir Paul McCartney.

Quote by Clint Eastwood. Reproduced by permission of Charles A. Scott, attorney-at-law for Clint Eastwood.

Quote by Martin Luther King Jr. Reprinted by arrangement with the Estate of Martin Luther King Jr., c/o Writers House as agent for the proprietor New York, NY. Copyright 1963 Dr. Martin Luther King Jr., copyright renewed 1991 Coretta Scott King.